Science Shocks!

Isabel Thomas
Illustrations by Fred Van Deele

Contents

Shocking science	2
Chemistry pioneer: Antoine Lavoisier	3
Stars in her eyes: Caroline Herschel	6
Electricity tamer: Michael Faraday	10
Globetrotting scientist: Charles Darwin	14
A killer discovery: Marie Curie	18
Moving the earth: Alfred Wegener	22
X-ray vision: Rosalind Franklin	26
Science still shocks	30
Glossary	31
Index	32

Shocking science

Who do you think of when you think of a hero? Is it a sports hero? An action hero? To me, a hero is someone who fights for what they believe in and changes the world for the better. A lot of my heroes are great scientists.

Science is all about testing ideas and making new discoveries. Sometimes these ideas and discoveries shock the world!

Many of the great scientific discoveries shocked the world. The scientists who made the discoveries were laughed at and ignored. Some lost their friends. Others were very poor and had to work in terrible conditions. Some even died because of the **experiments** they carried out.

Join me as I travel back in time to visit some of my favourite shocking scientists. I'll show you the **legacy** they have left for science today and what makes them real heroes. Lavoisier is first – let's go!

CHEMISTRY PIONEER:
Antoine Lavoisier

In the mid 1700s, chemistry was in a muddle. Luckily, Antoine Lavoisier came to the rescue and changed the way scientists worked forever.

Fact file

Born:	1743 in Paris, France
Worked in:	Chemistry
Died:	1794 in Paris, France
Interesting fact:	Lavoisier worked in many other areas, from collecting **tax** to making gunpowder! These jobs helped to pay for his scientific research.

What a mess!

18th-century scientists had lots of ideas about what substances were and why they changed. Experiments sometimes failed. This meant that no one could agree on what to call different chemicals! This may not sound a big deal but it caused a lot of problems.

A few of the problems

1. Many substances had lots of different names. For example, nitre (say: nigh-ter) and saltpetre (say: salt-peter) were actually both the same thing – an ingredient in gunpowder!
2. In the 1700s, scientists rarely bothered to weigh or measure the substances they mixed for experiments, or any new substances formed. This may not sound important but not **conducting** an experiment properly can cause big problems. It can affect your results, make experiments hard to repeat and could even be dangerous.
3. Many scientists thought burning happened when a secret substance came out of an object. They called it phlogiston (say: flow-gi-ston). They thought that phlogiston made heat and light. There was just one problem – it didn't exist.

During a lecture, Guillaume Rouelle caused an explosion by mixing nitric acid and turpentine. The audience escaped serious injury but a wig and a chimney were destroyed!

Lavoisier to the rescue!

Lavoisier wouldn't just accept official viewpoints; he wanted to explore why things were the way they were. One thing he wanted to find out was what really happened when something burned.

Antoine Lavoisier

I've come to watch Lavoisier experimenting with air – it's fascinating! He split the air into two gases, oxygen and nitrogen. He worked carefully, weighing and measuring everything. This helped him prove that the phlogiston **theory** was completely wrong!

The phlogiston experiment took 12 days and was first carried out in 1779.

Lavoisier's legacy

Lavoisier discovered that things burn when substances in them join with oxygen from the air. This **reaction** gives out heat and light. After this, scientists began to understand how other chemical reactions work.

Lavoisier also came up with a better way of naming chemicals and helped **establish** the metric system of measurements.

Science Souvenir

I'm bringing back a copy of *Elementary Treatise of Chemistry*, which Lavoisier helped to write more than 225 years ago. It described a brand new system for naming chemicals. The system was so good, it's still used today!

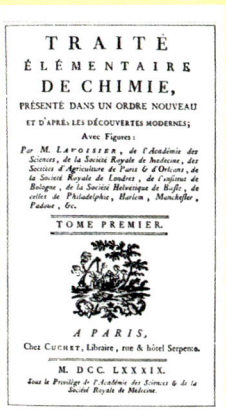

Fact file

Sadly, Lavoisier was **guillotined** during the **French Revolution** for his work as a tax collector.

STARS IN HER EYES:
Caroline Herschel

> *Over 250 years ago, the world was a very different place, especially if you were a woman. You could look at the stars but study them? No, way! Science was no place for a woman, or so they thought. That was until Caroline became the first ever paid female scientist.*

Fact file

Born:	1750 in Hanover, Germany
Worked in:	**Astronomy**
Other jobs:	Opera singer, musician
Died:	1848 in Hanover, Germany
Interesting fact:	Caroline was very ill as a child and grew to just 130 cm tall.

From scrubbing to stargazing

Caroline began to be interested in science when she went to live with her brother William in England. William loved stargazing and building telescopes. At first, Caroline looked after William's house and equipment. Then, when William became a famous astronomer, Caroline became his assistant. She helped William to find, track and record the position of stars, planets and other space objects.

Caroline Herschel

I'm visiting Observatory House in Windsor. This is where Caroline and William worked. Caroline earned £50 a year – the first time a woman had ever been paid for a job in science. In those days, astronomy was a dangerous job. Caroline had to crawl around huge telescopes in the dark. She often had accidents. Once she tripped over a metal hook hidden by snow. She wrote about it saying, "They could not lift me without leaving nearly two ounces of my flesh behind." Ouch!

William and Caroline built hundreds of telescopes to help them study the sky. The biggest was a 40-foot telescope. It weighed more than five cars and was the world's largest telescope for 50 years.

Objections to Caroline

Caroline soon began to make important discoveries of her own. Many male astronomers were shocked and angry. They wrote protest letters in scientific journals. Some suggested Caroline should be banned from using a telescope.

Science Souvenir

I've brought back this amazing letter from Caroline to her sister. It shows just how much she loved her work.

> William is away, and I am minding the heavens ... William says I have a way with numbers, so I handle all the necessary **reductions** and calculations. I also plan every night's observation schedule, for he says my **intuition** helps me turn the telescope to discover star cluster after star cluster.
>
> I have helped him polish the mirrors and lenses of our new telescope. It is the largest in existence. Can you imagine the thrill of turning it to some new corner of the heavens to see something never before seen from Earth? I actually like that he is busy with the Royal Society and his club, for when I finish my other work I can spend all night sweeping the heavens.

Caroline began to make observations on her own in 1782.

Shooting for the stars!

Caroline didn't let anything stop her! She discovered eight new comets and wrote huge catalogues about stars and other space objects. Two of these are still used today!

A comet is a chunk of ice and dust zooming around the Sun. When comets pass near the Sun, jets of gas and dust form 'tails' that can be seen from Earth.

Caroline's legacy

Caroline's science skills and hard work helped her become famous and win respect from other astronomers. In 1828, the Royal Astronomical Society presented her with their Gold Medal.

Caroline paved the way for other women to work in science. She thought that her name would be forgotten but it wasn't. An asteroid and a Moon crater have been named after her.

It was 168 years before another female scientist was awarded this medal.

ELECTRICITY TAMER:
Michael Faraday

Without Michael Faraday, we'd be living in the dark ... quite literally! He discovered how to use electricity to make things move and how to produce electricity using magnets. What's shocking is that he did all this with very little education!

Fact file

Born: 1791 in London, England
Childhood: Son of a blacksmith
Worked in: Physics
Died: 1897 in Hampton Court, England
Interesting fact: Faraday's first job was binding books. This used to be done by hand.

Teaching himself

In the early 1800s, science was a job for rich people who could afford to study at university. Faraday came from a poor family. He had to leave school and find work when he was 13. But Faraday loved to read. He taught himself all about science in the back of the shop where he worked.

Michael Faraday

Starting out

When he was 20, Faraday went to talks by a famous scientist called Humphrey Davy. Faraday wrote to Davy and got his first job in science.

No maths … no problem!

Maths is a really useful tool. It helps scientists discover how the world works. Faraday knew hardly any maths but he didn't let that stop him. He was brilliant at picturing how things might work.

In the early 1800s, no one used electricity as a source of power. Faraday changed this with his invention of the electric motor.

Science Souvenir

This is Faraday's first 'electric motor'. It doesn't look like today's motors – it's just a wire dipped into a pool of mercury metal with a magnet in the middle. When electricity was passed through the wire, something special happened – the wire started to **rotate** around the magnet!

The electricity creator

In 1831, Faraday took his work one step further and made the most important discovery of all. He worked out how to use magnets to create electricity. He passed a strong magnet through a coil of copper wire. The movement of the magnet created an electrical current in the wire. It really was that simple!

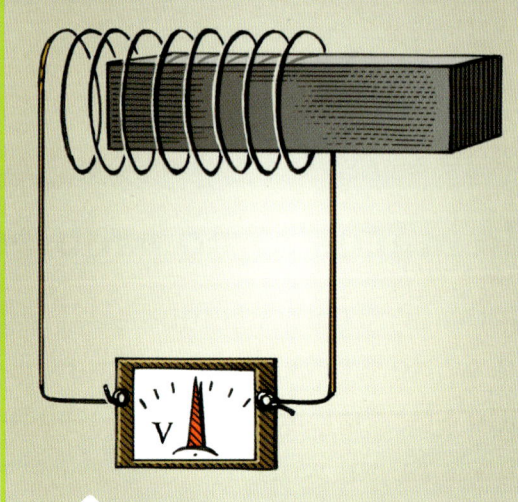

The faster the magnet moved and the more coils in the wire, the more electricity was created.

Power stations supply our homes with electricity, keeping the lights turned on and powering our computers and TVs. Today, power stations still produce electricity using the method that Faraday discovered.

Michael Faraday

Faraday was brilliant at explaining science to other people. I've come to one of his famous Christmas Lectures at the Royal Institute in London. Faraday started these in 1825. He wanted to inspire children to learn about science. The Christmas Lectures are still popular almost 200 years later. Every year, a famous scientist shows young people how amazing science is. You can watch them on television - thanks to Faraday!

Faraday presented a total of 19 Christmas Lecture series.

Faraday's legacy

Faraday's discoveries made it possible for us to understand and use electricity. His simple electric motor and idea about using magnets to create electricity helped other scientists to make brilliant discoveries that changed the world.

GLOBETROTTING SCIENTIST:
Charles Darwin

*An exciting round-the-world trip got Charles Darwin thinking. He realized that plants and animals change, or **evolve**, over time. His ideas shocked the world.*

Fact file

Born:	1809 in Shrewsbury, England
Worked as:	**Naturalist**
Other jobs:	Explorer
Died:	1882 in Downe, England
Interesting fact:	Darwin started training as a doctor. He gave up because he hated the sight of blood!

Voyage of the *Beagle*

Darwin didn't do very well at school but he was keen on science. He loved collecting beetles and other creatures. After deciding against a career as a doctor, he was invited on an adventure on board a ship called the *Beagle*. He sailed around the world for five years, collecting thousands of bugs, fossils and other **specimens**. On his return, he decided to become a naturalist.

Charles Darwin

Galapagos Islands
Found different **species** of plants, birds and tortoises on each island

Western South America
Shaken by an earthquake

Argentina
Collected fossils of giant extinct animals

Cocos Islands
Studied how coral islands formed

Darwin's voyage

Falklands
Fascinated by the Falkland Island wolf

Brazil
Amazed by strange tropical plants and creatures

South Africa
Collected many unusual rocks

Australia
Puzzled by strange creatures, such as the duck-billed platypus

Spot the difference

Back in England, Darwin thought about all the plants and animals he'd seen. He puzzled over the animals of the Galapagos Islands, far out in the Pacific Ocean. Each island was home to similar animals, such as finches and Giant tortoises. However, the birds and tortoises of each island had different body features. Why had they developed in different ways?

Darwin noticed that the Galapagos finches had different shaped beaks.

I'm visiting Down House in Kent, where Darwin lived and worked. He didn't just make his discoveries when travelling. He also kept pigeons, to study how **breeding** could change a species.

Darwin bred all the UK breeds of pigeons to prove they were one species.

Darwin's big idea

Darwin realized that each animal's body had changed to suit the place they lived. The animals that were best suited to living on each island were the ones who were most likely to survive. They passed their features on to their babies. Darwin called this process 'natural selection'. His theory was that, over time, each species changes, or evolves, as it adapts to life in a particular place.

Darwin spent 20 years working on his ideas before publishing his book. It was called *On the Origin of Species*. Darwin knew that his new theory would upset many people. He was right. His new, groundbreaking ideas caused **uproar** and were not accepted for many years.

Science Souvenir

Some people were furious with Darwin. Others made fun of him. I've brought back this newspaper cartoon which appeared in *Punch* Magazine in May 1861.

Darwin's legacy

Today, Darwin's theories are an important part of how biologists, and many others, view the world.

A KILLER DISCOVERY:
Marie Curie

Imagine discovering a new material with strange powers that could change the world! Marie Curie did this. She became the first person to win two Nobel prizes. Then came a shock – the work that made her a celebrity also killed her.

Fact file

Born: 1867 in Warsaw, Poland
Worked in: Physics and chemistry
Died: 1934 in Paris, France
Interesting fact: In the 1800s, women were not allowed to study at university in Poland so Marie moved to France. She got two degrees in physics and mathematics.

Strange rays

Marie began studying a metal called uranium (say: you-ray-nee-um). It gave out invisible rays that passed straight through objects. They also made air behave in strange ways. Marie called this 'radioactivity'. She was sure that there must be other materials that gave out these powerful rays.

Marie Curie

Rock samples

Marie's husband Pierre was also a scientist. He helped Marie to search for these mysterious materials. They searched deep inside rocks, before taking the samples back to the **laboratory** for analysis. Laboratories were not the safe, high-tech places they are today. The work was difficult and dangerous.

> It was exhausting work to move the containers about, to transfer the liquids and to stir for hours at a time, with an iron bar, the boiling material in the cast iron basin.
>
> Marie Curie

Hidden in the rocks

Working together, Pierre and Marie discovered two new **radioactive** substances – polonium (say: po-low-nee-um) and radium (say: ray-dee-um).

1. Marie named polonium after the country where she was born.

2. Radium was named after the rays it emitted.

Prize winners

Marie and Pierre won a Nobel prize for their discoveries. They both became famous as a result. Sadly, Pierre was killed in a road accident just a few years later but Marie kept working hard. She won a second Nobel prize for working out how to get pure radium metal out of the rocks it was found in. This meant it could be studied and used for new things – such as medicine.

Uraninite is a source of uranium.

Fact file

The Nobel prize is an international award. It is given to people who have made major advances in science or culture. The winner receives a gold medal, a diploma and money.

Marie and Pierre Curie won the Physics award in 1903, just two years after the very first awards took place. Marie's second award in 1911 was given in the **field** of chemistry. She was the first person to win two Nobel prizes.

Science Souvenir

I've brought back this copy of a French newspaper from 1901. Marie and Pierre are on the cover! It shows how famous they were.

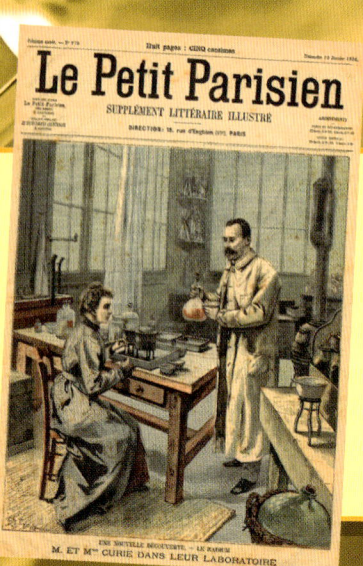

Marie Curie

Marie Curie at work in her laboratory in the College de Sorbonne, where she was the first female professor.

Shh! We need to be quiet. I'm in Marie's laboratory, watching her work. I'm standing well back so I'm not affected by the radiation! Back then, no one knew how dangerous radioactivity was. Marie handled radioactive materials all day long. She began to feel sick and tired all the time. She eventually died of cancer, caused by the chemicals she worked with.

Marie's legacy

Marie's work helped the world to understand radioactivity. Today it is used for many different things, from making electricity in power stations to finding and treating diseases in hospitals. Marie was the first to experiment with using it to treat cancer.

MOVING THE EARTH:
Alfred Wegener

In the early 20th century, the world was changing quickly. At least the ground beneath people's feet was stable! That was until Alfred Wegener shocked them with a new idea.

Fact file

Born:	1880 in Berlin, Germany
Studied:	Astronomy
Worked as:	**Meteorologist**
Hobbies:	Exploring the Arctic; flying hot air balloons
Died:	1930 in Greenland
Interesting fact:	In 1906, Wegener and his brother set a world record for 52 hours in a hot air balloon.

Fossil mystery

In 1911, Wegener read that fossils that were similar to each other had been found either side of the Atlantic Ocean – thousands of kilometres apart. Most scientists thought huge 'land bridges' had once joined the continents, letting animals walk from one to the other. Wegener thought differently and came up with the theory of continental drift.

Alfred Wegener

Continental drift

Wegener thought that the Earth's continents were once joined together in a supercontinent. He thought parts of this had gradually moved apart over millions of years.

Gathering evidence

Wegener thought continental drift was the best way to explain three strange things:

1. The coasts of North and South America 'fitted' the coasts of Africa and Europe.

The world map seemed like a giant jigsaw puzzle to Wegener.

2. Similar fossils were found in very different areas of the world. Wegener thought this showed that the land had once moved.

Mesosaurus lizard fossils are found on both sides of the Atlantic Ocean.

3. Mountains on different continents were very similar. Wegener suggested they were once part of the same mountain range.

Rock layers in the Appalachian Mountains match rock layers in the Scottish Highlands.

"I've come to see Wegener working on his theory of continental drift. He was dedicated to his ideas even though most scientists said they were ridiculous. He was challenging the popular ideas of the time and I really admire his dedication and courage!"

Wegener called the supercontinent Pangaea, which means 'all the Earth'.

The supercontinent Pangaea

The continents as they are now.

Fact file

Wegener loved exploring the Arctic on foot. He died on his third expedition to Greenland.

Mystery solved?

In 1912, Wegener put forward his new theory. He had collected lots of evidence but there was one big problem. He could not explain HOW such huge pieces of land could move apart. He had no evidence that the land was still moving.

Alfred Wegener

New evidence

Many years after Wegener's death, people became interested in Wegener's ideas again. When scientists explored the oceans, they found huge mountain ranges underwater. They realized that the seafloor was moving apart in these places. They decided that this could explain how the continents moved.

In the 1960s, scientists proved that the Earth's crust is split up into large pieces, or plates, which move around very slowly. This showed how continental drift was possible.

Two plates sliding past each other have formed California's San Andreas Fault. They move around 5 cm every year. This makes the area around the San Andreas Fault vulnerable to earthquakes.

When plates move towards each other, the edges can push up to form mountains. This is how the Himalayas were created.

Wegener's legacy

30 years after Wegener died, he was proved right! His theory is the basis for our current ideas on **plate tectonics**. Wegener got there first because he was not scared to challenge old ideas – even if the new ones were shocking.

X-RAY VISION:
Rosalind Franklin

What makes you, you? Why do you grow in a different way from a flower, a frog, or your friends? Rosalind Franklin was a brilliant scientist who helped to find the answer to those questions. She used X-rays to look at things really closely. Shockingly, she never got the credit she deserved.

Fact file

Born:	1920 in London, England
Worked in:	Chemistry
Died:	1958 in London, England
Interesting fact:	Franklin decided to become a scientist when she was 15. This was a brave decision for a woman in the 1930s when many women didn't work.

X-ray expert

Franklin was one of the best people in the world at using X-rays to take photographs of crystals. Her pictures showed things we could never see with our eyes. They showed how crystals were structured and let us see the tiny atoms within them.

Rosalind Franklin

Franklin started working as a researcher at Kings College London in 1951.

I've come to visit Rosalind at work in Kings College, London. She was brilliant at her job, although she didn't always get on with her colleagues, which caused some problems.

DNA study

One of the substances Rosalind was studying was **DNA**. This is found inside every living thing. It tells our bodies how to grow and makes each of us what we are. DNA was originally discovered in the 19th century but no one really knew much about it. In the 1950s, scientists around the world were racing to discover what DNA was made of and how it worked.

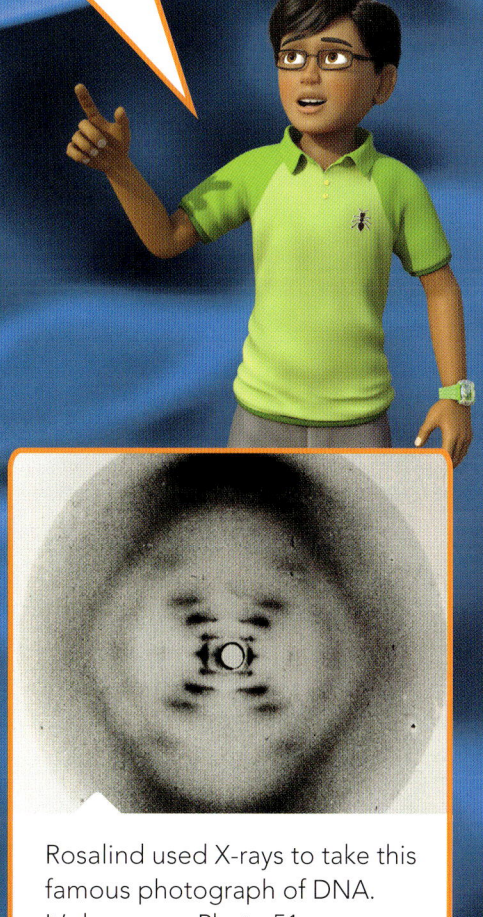

Rosalind used X-rays to take this famous photograph of DNA. It's known as Photo 51.

A big discovery

Without Rosalind knowing, her colleague Maurice Wilkins showed Photo 51 to a scientist called James Watson. Watson and his colleague Francis Crick had been trying to understand DNA for ages. Rosalind's photograph and notes helped Watson and Crick to see its structure. They worked out that DNA is shaped like a twisted ladder. They called this shape a 'double helix'. Watson said, "The instant I saw the picture, my mouth fell open and my pulse began to race …".

Nobel prize winners James D. Watson and Francis Crick.

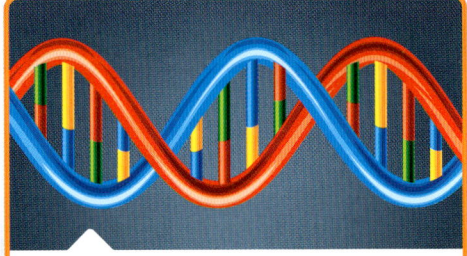

This is a model of DNA. The bits that look like rungs carry the code for building living things. The DNA in your body contains all the instructions for making you!

Science Souvenir

I'm bringing back this page from Rosalind's notebook. It shows that she was working out the structure of DNA herself!

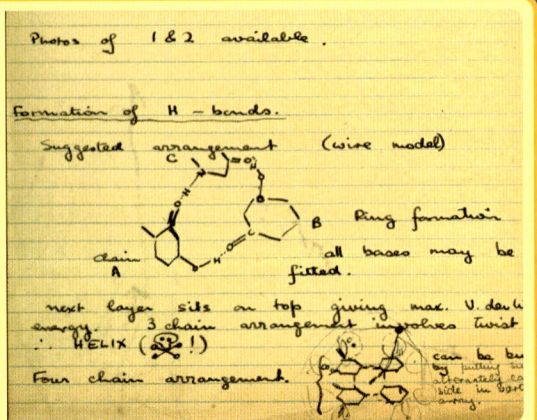

Missing out on a prize

Watson and Crick quickly became world famous. They won many awards and prizes for unlocking the secret of DNA. In 1962, Watson, Crick and Wilkins shared the top award in science – a Nobel prize. Sadly, Franklin had died in 1958. Nobel prizes are only awarded to living people, so she was not mentioned. Her important work on DNA was in danger of being forgotten.

James Watson and Francis Crick receiving their Nobel prizes in Stockholm in 1962.

Fact file

Rosalind also made brilliant discoveries about coal and viruses.

Franklin's legacy

The secret of DNA was one of the world's greatest scientific discoveries. It helped scientists to understand life and changed biology forever. 30 years after Franklin died, people began to realize what a big part she had played in this.

Today, awards, science laboratories and buildings are named after Rosalind Franklin.

Science *still* shocks

Wow, what a whirlwind tour. We have seen some of the most shocking science moments in history! Mind you, while it might seem like the most shocking scientific discoveries are behind us, actually, scientists are still making amazing discoveries.

There are still so many theories to be tested and hidden worlds to explore. Some scientists want to find out about the bottom of the deepest ocean, others want to explore the furthest reaches of outer space. There are always more science secrets to uncover.

Would you like to work in a futuristic lab?

So it seems as if science still has the ability to shock us. Many of today's discoveries can seem incredible and a bit scary. However, scientists today must continue to pave the way for potentially life-changing discoveries.

I've learned that if you want to be successful, you need to believe in your ideas and never give up – even if your work shocks the world! Who knows, maybe one day you'll make a shocking scientific discovery, too.

Glossary

astronomy — the study of stars, planets and other objects in outer space

breeding — mating animals to produce offspring

conducting — carrying out

DNA — the substance in our bodies that carries the code for 'building' us

establish — to bring about; create

evolve — to change and develop over time

experiments — controlled scientific tests

field — a branch of knowledge

French Revolution — when the power to rule was taken away from the French monarchy (1789-99)

guillotined — killed by being beheaded with a heavy blade

intuition — the ability to know something without any proof or evidence

laboratory — a place with special equipment for carrying out scientific tests

legacy — something that comes from someone in the past

naturalist — someone who studies plants and animals as they live in nature

plate tectonics — a theory explaining the structure of the Earth's crust

radioactive — giving off rays of energy or particles by the breaking apart of certain atoms

reaction — a chemical process when substances act on each other

reduction — analysis of complex things to make them simpler

species — a group of creatures that can breed with each other

specimens — a sample of a plant, animal or mineral

tax — the money people have to pay to the government

theory — a system of ideas to try and explain something

uproar — when people are upset or angry about something

Index

astronomy	6-7, 22
chemistry	3, 5, 18, 20, 26
comets	9
DNA	27-29
electricity	10-13, 21
Galapagos Islands	15, 16
gunpowder	3, 4
Himalayas	25
magnets	10, 12-13
mercury	11
nitrogen	5
Nobel prizes	18, 20, 29
oxygen	5
phlogiston	4-5
power	11, 12, 18, 21
radiation	21
Royal Astronomical Society	9
San Andreas Fault	25
scientists	2-6, 9, 11, 13, 14, 19, 22, 25-29, 30
stars	6, 8, 9
substances	3-5, 19, 26-27
telescopes	6-8
uranium	18